AF680338

# The Architecture of a Mind

Ja'Shaun Coley

Published by Ja'Shaun Coley, 2026.

While every precaution has been taken in the preparation of this book, the publisher assumes no responsibility for errors or omissions, or for damages resulting from the use of the information contained herein.

THE ARCHITECTURE OF A MIND

**First edition. January 8, 2026.**

Copyright © 2026 Ja'Shaun Coley.

ISBN: 979-8233365379

Written by Ja'Shaun Coley.

# Table of Contents

# 1. The High-Speed Ghost (High-Functioning Anxiety)

They call it "doing well." They see the clean shoes, the turned-in assignments, the "yes sir," the "no ma'am," and the way I hold the door open with a smile that looks like it was painted on by a master. They see a fire and call it a glow. But they don't feel the heat. High-functioning is just a polite way of saying I'm running a marathon on a broken ankle and nobody noticed because I'm winning the race. It's the noise. That's the part they don't tell you. It isn't a single scream; it's a million tiny whispers that keep my heart beating too fast. It's the constant "what if" playing on a loop like a scratched record in the back of my skull. It's checking the lock four times not because I'm forgetful, but because I don't trust the world to stay outside once the sun goes down. I am a ghost in a high-speed chase with myself. I perform because I'm terrified of what happens if I stop. If I stop moving, the thoughts catch up. If I stop achieving, the worth disappears. So I keep the engine screaming. I keep the calendar full. I let them tell me how "inspired" they are by my drive, while I'm behind the wheel praying for a red light that never comes. It's exhausting to be the person everyone relies on when you're the person you can't even sit still with for five minutes.

# 2. The Calendar of Clouds (Seasonal Depression)

The sun starts leaving work early and suddenly, so do I. It's a slow robbery. The light retreats, and my marrow follows. They call it the "winter blues," like it's just a color you can wash off in the shower, but it feels more like a thickening of the blood. It's the way the air turns sharp and suddenly the bed has a gravity that the floor can't compete with. I'm not just tired; I'm weighted down by the gray. I am a quiet house with the heat turned off.

I watch the trees go bare and I feel a kinship with the skeletons in the yard. We are both waiting for a permission slip to breathe again. You can't tell a flower to bloom in a blizzard, so why do they expect me to smile when the sky has been the color of wet concrete for a month? It's the silence of the season. The world goes muffled under the cold, and my thoughts go muffled with it. I'm mourning a version of myself that was loud and bright in July, a version that didn't need three layers of blankets just to feel human. I'm hibernating in a world that doesn't believe in rest, trying to remember what the sun felt like on the back of my neck while I stare at a ceiling that feels three inches lower than it did last week. I am waiting for the thaw. I am holding my breath until the earth decides to wake up, praying that I haven't forgotten how to wake up with it.

# 3. The Redline (Burnout)

I ran out of "yes" three weeks ago. Now, I am just a hollow echo of a person, repeating the motions because the machine doesn't know how to stop. Burnout isn't being tired; being tired is fixed by a nap. Burnout is when your soul feels like a used-up matchstick. You strike and strike, but there's no sulfur left. Only the scrape of wood against stone. I am a battery that won't hold a charge. I plug into the wall, I sleep for ten hours, and I wake up at 4%.

It's the guilt of the "empty" light on the dashboard while everyone is asking for a ride. I'm staring at the emails, the texts, the chores—and they look like mountains I'm expected to climb with no shoes. I didn't crash in a spectacular explosion; I just evaporated. I became a ghost in my own life. My favorite songs sound like noise. My favorite foods taste like cardboard. I am redlining the engine just to stay at the speed limit, and I can smell the smoke coming from under the hood. I want to pull over. I want to turn the key and hear the silence, but the world keeps shouting that I'm "so productive." They love the output, but they don't see the input is zero. I am a hollowed-out tree, still standing, but waiting for a wind strong enough to finally let me lie down.

# 4. The 3:00 AM Theater (Night Terrors)

The sun goes down and the curtains rise. My bed is supposed to be a sanctuary, but sometimes it's a battlefield where I'm the only one unarmed. It's the jolt. That lightning strike in the chest that wakes you up before the dream even finishes. You're scanning the shadows for a ghost that doesn't have a name, heart hammering against your ribs like a bird in a cage that's on fire. Adrenaline is a cruel alarm clock.

I'm awake, but my brain is still stuck in the "run." I'm touching the walls to make sure they're solid, counting my breaths to remind my lungs they belong to me and not the nightmare. The world is silent, but inside, it's a riot. Every shadow looks like a hand reaching out. Every floorboard creak sounds like a threat. I'm a soldier in a war that ended hours ago, but my body hasn't received the message yet. I sit there in the dark, sweating, waiting for the logic to return. I'm waiting for the morning to come and negotiate a peace treaty between my mind and the dark. It's hard to trust the sleep when the sleep is where the monsters live. I'm tired of being afraid of the one place I'm supposed to find rest.

## 5. The Performance (The Mask)

I am an architect of the "I'm good." I build it every morning in the mirror. I check the corners of my mouth to make sure they aren't sagging. I check my eyes to make sure the "tired" isn't leaking out. Social camouflage is a survival skill. If I show you the mess, you'll try to clean it, and I don't want to be a chore. I don't want to be the "problem" in the room. So I put on the mask. I play the part of the person you expect to see—the funny one, the strong one, the one who has it all figured out.

It's heavy, wearing another person's skin over your own, but it's safer than letting you see the cracks in the foundation. I spend the whole day adjusting the fit, making sure the mask doesn't slip when the conversation gets too deep. But when I get home, when the door is locked and the lights are low, the mask comes off, and I realize I don't even recognize the face underneath anymore. I've been the character for so long that the actor is missing. I'm tired of the performance. I'm tired of the applause for a version of me that doesn't exist. I want to be messy. I want to be unfinished. I want to be able to say "I'm not okay" without feeling like I'm failing the audience.

# 6. The Radio Static (Brain Fog)

I'm looking for a word that's sitting on the tip of my tongue, but the map is missing. Brain fog is like trying to drive through a cloud of smoke with no headlights. I know I'm in there somewhere, but the connection is lagging. I'm staring at the grocery list like it's written in a dead language. I'm walking into rooms and forgetting why I exist. It's the static on a radio station you used to love. You can hear the melody faintly, but the noise is too loud to let you sing along.

It's frustrating to feel your own intelligence slipping through your fingers like sand. I want to be sharp. I want to be present. But instead, I am floating in a gray middle-ground where thoughts go to die. I start a sentence and lose the ending halfway through. I look at my friends and it takes an extra second for their names to click. It's not that I'm not trying; it's that the signal is weak. I'm a computer with too many tabs open, spinning the loading wheel while the world waits for a response. I just want the sky to clear. I want to feel the "snap" of a quick thought again. But for now, I am just navigating the fog, hoping I don't bump into too many things before the sun comes back out.

# 7. The Sudden Ocean (Panic Attacks)

The room didn't get smaller; my lungs just forgot how to expand. It's a glitch in the software. One minute I'm standing in line for coffee, thinking about my day, and the next, the floor is made of water and I'm forgetting how to swim. My throat is a narrow hallway and everyone is trying to leave at once. It's the terror of a threat that isn't there—a ghost with a knife standing right behind me, even though I'm in a brightly lit room.

A false alarm that rings so loud you can't hear your own common sense. My hands are shaking, my vision is tunneling, and my brain is screaming that this is the end. *Breathe*, they say. As if I haven't been trying to do that since the moment I was born. As if I've suddenly forgotten the most basic requirement of being alive. Every breath feels like it's being filtered through a straw. I'm clawing at the air, trying to find enough oxygen to prove I'm not dying. And then, as quickly as it came, the tide goes out. I'm left shivering, soaked in sweat, wondering how I can go back to "normal" when I know how easily the ocean can swallow me whole in the middle of a Tuesday afternoon.

## 8. The Crowded Room (Chronic Loneliness)

You can be surrounded by a thousand people and still feel like an island. Loneliness isn't about the absence of bodies; it's about the absence of being seen. I am a frequency that no one is tuned into. I'm talking, but the words are falling into the gap between us like stones in a well. It's the feeling of being the only one at the party who didn't get the script. Everyone else is connecting like Legos, snapping together with ease, while I'm a puzzle piece from a different box entirely.

I smile when they smile. I laugh when the room laughs. But inside, I am screaming for someone to look me in the eye and see the "help" I'm hiding. I'm a ghost haunting my own social life, watching the world move in slow motion from behind a thick pane of glass. I go home and the silence is a physical weight, but the "noise" of being misunderstood is worse. I'm tired of being "fine" for people who don't care to ask what's underneath. I'm looking for my echo. I'm looking for the person who hears the static and recognizes it as music. Until then, I am just a quiet observer in a very loud world.

## 9. The Out-of-Body Experience (Dissociation)

I am watching myself from the ceiling. I see the top of my head, the way I'm nodding, the way I'm holding the glass—but I'm not in the seat. Dissociation is the ultimate "unplug." When the world gets too loud or the feelings get too sharp, my mind just leaves the building. I'm a passenger in my own body, watching a movie of my life but I can't reach the controls. I'm pressing the buttons, but the character isn't moving.

Everything feels "almost" real. The colors are a little too bright, or maybe they're too dull. The voices sound like they're coming from underwater. I'm touching the table to see if it's solid, but my fingers don't feel like they belong to me. It's a survival mechanism that feels like a prison. I'm safe from the pain because I'm not "there," but I'm also missing the joy. I'm waiting for the tether to pull me back down to earth, waiting for the "thud" of landing back in my own skin. I want to be present, even if the "present" hurts. Being a ghost is lonely. I want to feel the weight of my own bones again.

# 10. The Weight of Silence

Sometimes the loudest thing in the house is what I'm not saying. It's the "I'm fine" that actually means "I'm drowning but I don't want to get your floor wet." Silence is a heavy coat. It protects you from the wind, but it makes it hard to move. I'm keeping secrets from people who love me because I don't know how to put the pain into a sentence that doesn't sound like a scream. I don't want to see the pity in their eyes. I don't want to be the "unbroken" thing that finally snapped.

So I stay quiet. I let the silence grow until it's a wall between us. I'm screaming on the inside, a high-pitched frequency that only I can hear, while on the outside I'm just "tired." I'm holding onto the words until they turn into stones in my stomach. I'm terrified that if I open my mouth, everything will come pouring out at once—the grief, the fear, the anger—and I won't be able to stop it. So I swallow it back down. I choose the weight over the risk. I choose the wall over the window. I am a vault with a forgotten combination, and I am the only one trapped inside.

## 11. The Unlearning (Unlearning Trauma)

I am digging up the garden of my mind and realizing most of the plants are weeds I was told were flowers. Unlearning is harder than learning. I have to convince my heart that the footsteps in the hallway aren't a threat. I have to tell my nervous system that the silence isn't "the calm before the storm"—it's just peace. I'm breaking the bones of my old habits so they can heal straight this time. It hurts to grow. It hurts to admit that the "strength" I was proud of was actually just a defense mechanism. I'm unlearning the idea that I have to earn my right to exist. I'm unlearning the belief that being "useful" is the same as being "loved." I'm looking at the blueprint of my personality and realizing how much of it was built on fear. It's messy work, getting down into the dirt and pulling things up by the root. Sometimes I want to just cover it back up and pretend the garden is fine. But I want real flowers. I want a mind that isn't a minefield. So I keep digging. I keep unlearning. I'm shedding the old skin so the new one can finally breathe.

## 12. The Uninvited Guest (Intrusive Thoughts)

My brain is a theater that sometimes plays horror movies without my permission. An intrusive thought is a spark in a dry forest. It's the "what if you just..." that makes your stomach turn. It's the worst version of yourself whispering in your ear, trying to convince you that you're a monster. It's not who I am, but it's what my mind does when it's trying to "protect" me by imagining every possible catastrophe.

It's exhausting to argue with a voice that sounds like your own but says things you'd never dream of doing. I have to learn to look at the thought and say: *You are a guest, but you don't live here. You can sit on the porch, but I'm not letting you in.* I'm learning to stop fighting the thoughts and start observing them. If I fight them, they get stronger. If I watch them, they eventually get bored and leave. I am not my thoughts. I am the space where the thoughts happen. I'm trying to keep the theater clean, even when the projector glitches and shows me something I didn't ask to see.

## 13. The Fraud (Imposter Syndrome)

I'm waiting for the tap on the shoulder. The one that says: *We figured it out. We know you're just pretending. Please leave through the back door.* Imposter syndrome is the shadow that follows every success. I didn't "earn" it; I just got lucky. I'm not "talented"; I'm just a good liar. I'm looking at my own achievements like they belong to someone else. I'm a thief in my own life, convinced that any moment now, the sirens will start and they'll take it all back.

I'm over-preparing, over-working, and over-thinking because I'm terrified of making one mistake that reveals the "truth." Even when I win, I feel like I've cheated. I'm looking at the people around me and thinking they all have a secret manual for life that I missed out on. I'm an actor who forgot the lines but is still being told I'm doing a great job. I'm trying to learn how to own my space. I'm trying to believe that I'm allowed to be here, even if I don't feel 100% ready. I'm trying to remember that everyone else is probably just as scared and confused as I am, they're just better at hiding the "pretend."

# 14. The Empty Chair (Grief)

Grief isn't a mountain you climb; it's an ocean you learn to sail. Some days the water is calm, and I can almost forget the loss. I can go through the motions and even laugh a little. Then a song plays, or I smell a certain type of wood, or I see a shadow that looks like them, and the wave hits. I'm underwater again. My lungs are full of the past. Grief is the price we pay for love, and some days, the bill feels too high to pay.

I'm carrying around a person-shaped hole in my life, trying to figure out how to be whole when a piece of the foundation is gone. You don't "get over" it; you just get used to the weight. You learn how to walk with the limp. I find myself wanting to call them, wanting to share a joke, and then the realization hits like a physical punch to the gut. They aren't there. The chair is empty. The world keeps turning, which feels like an insult. How can the sun still rise when the light is gone? I'm learning to live in the "after," finding ways to honor the memory without letting the sadness drown out the beauty of what we had.

# 15. The Family Table (The Stigma)

In my house, we don't talk about the "mind." We talk about "getting over it." We talk about "praying it away" or "manning up." The stigma is a second layer of the sickness. It's the shame of needing help in a culture that values "strength" and "resilience" above all else. I'm trying to tell my family that my brain is sick, and they're telling me I'm just lazy or I need to get out more. It's lonely, being the one to break the cycle of silence.

I'm the one saying the words they've been swallowing for generations. I'm the one looking at the history of "nervous breakdowns" and "difficult personalities" in my family and calling it what it actually is: undiagnosed pain. It's hard to heal when the people you love think your healing is a sign of weakness. I'm sitting at the table, eating my dinner, and feeling like I'm from another planet. I want to tell them that it's okay to not be okay. I want to tell them that therapy isn't for "crazy" people; it's for brave people. But for now, I'm just the one holding the torch, hoping the light eventually reaches the rest of them.

# 16. The Funhouse Mirror (Body Dysmorphia)

I don't see what you see. I see a map of flaws. I see a body that feels like an enemy territory I'm trying to negotiate with. Body dysmorphia is a liar with a very loud voice and a magnifying glass. It takes the smallest thing—a curve, a line, a shadow—and blows it up until it's all I can see. I'm checking every reflection like I'm looking for a stranger who broke into my house. I'm trying to remember that my body is a vessel, not a display case.

It's the house I live in, and I'm tired of hating the walls. I spend so much time trying to "fix" the exterior that I forget there's a person living inside who needs kindness. I look at photos and I don't recognize the person smiling back. I feel like I'm wearing a costume that doesn't fit right. I'm trying to learn how to see myself with "soft eyes"—the way I see my friends. I wouldn't pick them apart like this. I wouldn't tell them they aren't enough because of a number on a scale or the way their jeans fit. I'm trying to sign a peace treaty with the mirror. I'm trying to remember that I am more than the sum of my parts.

## 17. The Gray Room (Emotional Numbness)

I would trade this for sadness in a heartbeat. Numbness isn't peace; it's a void. It's the feeling of watching your favorite movie and feeling absolutely nothing. It's looking at a sunset and seeing only physics and light-waves. I'm a ghost in a world of color. I'm trying to feel the edges of my own life, but everything is wrapped in thick, gray plastic. I'm pushing against the world, but there's no resistance.

I'm a pilot who lost the controls. I can see the clouds, I can see the ground, but I can't feel the tilt of the wings. I'm waiting for the spark. I'm waiting for the "ouch" or the "aha" or the "yes." I'm trying to trigger a response—any response. I'm watching people cry at weddings or scream at sports games and I'm jealous of their intensity. I am a hollowed-out bell that won't ring. I'm just waiting to be human again. I'm waiting for the weather to change inside my chest. I know the feelings are still there, somewhere under the ice. I'm just waiting for the sun to get hot enough to melt it.

## 18. The Line in the Sand (Setting Boundaries)

"No" is a complete sentence, but it feels like a crime. I've been a people-pleaser for so long that setting a boundary feels like starting a war. I've been the "yes" man, the one who carries everyone else's bags, the one who stays late and smiles through the resentment. But I'm realizing that if I don't build a fence, people will walk all over the garden until there's nothing left to grow.

I'm learning that my time is mine. My energy is mine. My peace is not for sale. It's uncomfortable, watching people get upset when they can no longer use you for their own convenience. You see their true colors when you stop being a "yes." But that's how you know the boundary was needed. I'm drawing the line in the sand, and I'm not apologizing for the space I'm taking up. I'm learning that "selfless" is often just another word for "exhausted." I'm choosing to be whole instead of being a collection of pieces I've given away to everyone else.

## 19. The Small Version (Inner Child Work)

There is a ten-year-old version of me living in my chest, and he's still scared. He's the one who reacts when someone raises their voice, even if it's not at him. He's the one who feels like he's in trouble when everything is actually fine. He's the one who still thinks he has to be perfect to be safe. Inner child work is about going back and being the parent I needed then. It's about looking that little version of me in the eye and saying: *It's okay. You don't have to carry the world anymore. I've got the wheel.* I'm holding his hand while we walk through the dark parts of the past. I'm telling him that his feelings are valid, that his anger is okay, and that he's allowed to just be a kid. I'm protecting him from the ghosts he couldn't fight off back then. It's strange, being both the protector and the protected. But as I heal him, I heal myself. We're growing up together, finally, on our own terms.

# 20. The Shadow of the Cliff (The Fear of Relapse)

I'm doing better, and that's the scariest part. When you're at the bottom, there's nowhere to fall. You're already on the ground. But when you're on the mountain, the view is beautiful and the drop is terrifying. I'm constantly checking my "symptoms" like a hypochondriac of the soul. Is this just a bad Tuesday, or is the "Big Dark" coming back to claim me? Every time I feel a little bit of sadness, I panic, thinking it's the beginning of the end.

I'm looking over my shoulder, waiting for the shadow to catch up. I'm terrified that I'm just in a "good phase" and the "real me" is the one who can't get out of bed. But I'm learning to trust the sun again, even though I know the clouds still exist. I'm learning that a bad day isn't a bad life. A slip isn't a fall. I'm learning to live in the "now" instead of the "what if it happens again." I'm building a safety net of habits and people, so that if I do fall, I won't go all the way to the bottom. I'm learning that I am stronger than the fear of my own shadow.

## 21. The First Word (Choosing Therapy)

I sat in a chair and paid a stranger to help me hold my own heart. The first session felt like an admission of defeat. I felt like I was walking into the principal's office to confess that I couldn't handle being a human being. But as the words started coming out, I realized it was actually the first day of the revolution. Therapy isn't "fixing" you; it's getting a second pair of eyes to help you look at the map you've been trying to read in the dark.

It's the relief of saying the "unsayable" and realizing the room didn't explode. I didn't get kicked out. The sky didn't fall. I'm finally putting the luggage down and looking at what's inside—the old grudges, the dusty fears, the things I've been carrying since I was five. I'm sorting through it all, deciding what to keep and what to throw away. It's hard work, and sometimes I leave feeling more tired than when I arrived, but it's a "good" tired. It's the tired of a house being renovated. I'm tearing down the walls that were blocking the light. I'm finally building a home I can actually live in.

# 22. The Ink vs. The Cloud (Writing as Self-Medication)

I used to reach for the vape when the air got too heavy. I'd take that long pull, wait for the buzz, and watch the cloud vanish into the ceiling. It was a temporary reset, a digital exhale for a soul that forgot how to breathe on its own. It was a way to make the world "blurry" for a second so I didn't have to look at the sharp edges of my own thoughts. But the cloud always disappeared, and the weight always stayed. The "fix" was as hollow as the vapor.

So I traded the plastic for a pen. I traded the vapor for the ink. Now, when the pressure builds and the room starts to feel small, I don't exhale it away—I bleed it onto the page. The vape was a "hide." The writing is a "find." Writing doesn't make the thoughts disappear; it makes them manageable. It gives them a shape. The ink stays where I put it. It holds the weight so my chest doesn't have to. I am no longer trying to disappear into the smoke; I am trying to appear on the paper. I am finding my voice in the scratches of the pen, finding a way to breathe that doesn't involve a battery. I am writing my way out of the dark, one word at a time.

# 23. Unconditional (Unconditional Self-Acceptance)

I am done with the "if"s. I've spent my whole life negotiating with myself. *I'll love myself if I lose ten pounds. I'll love myself if I get the straight A's. I'll love myself if I can go a week without a panic attack.* I've been holding my own affection hostage, waiting for a perfection that's never going to come. No more. I am choosing me, as I am, right now, in the middle of the mess, with the laundry on the floor and the thoughts in a knot.

Unconditional means there are no requirements. I am a human being, not a "to-do" list. I am accepting the parts of me that are loud, the parts that are broken, and the parts that are still under construction. I am my own permanent residence. I am the only person I am guaranteed to be with from the first breath to the last. I might as well love the decor. I'm stopping the war against myself. I'm signing the peace treaty. I am enough—not because of what I do, but because of who I am. I am unconditional. I am whole. I am home.

## 24. The Letter of Release (Forgiveness)

Forgiveness isn't saying what they did was okay. It's not an invitation for them to come back and do it again. It's simply saying: *I'm not going to carry your debt in my pocket anymore.* It's for me, not for them. I'm tired of being angry. Anger is a hot coal that I'm holding, waiting to throw it at someone else, but I'm the one getting burned. I'm the one with the scarred hands.

I'm letting go. I'm opening my hand and letting the coal drop. I'm choosing my peace over my "right" to be bitter. I'm realizing that holding onto the grudge is like drinking poison and expecting the other person to die. I'm releasing the version of the past where things went differently. I'm accepting the reality of what happened so I can move into the reality of what's next. I am free because I decided to be. I am taking back the energy I was using to hate them and I'm using it to love myself instead. The cage is open, and I'm the one who had the key the whole time.

# 25. The Victory of the Water (Small Wins/The Shower Essay)

Today, I took a shower. That sounds small to you, but to me, it was a battle. On the days when the "Heavy" is winning, the simple act of standing under the water and washing the "yesterday" off your skin is a heroic feat. The gravity of the bed is strong, but I was stronger. I celebrated the victory. I celebrated the clean clothes. I celebrated the fact that I brushed my teeth and looked myself in the eye for three seconds.

We spend so much time waiting for the big trophies—the graduations, the promotions, the big "I'm healed" moments—that we forget to cheer for the small ones. But the small ones are the ones that keep us alive. Life is made of small wins. It's the decision to make the bed. It's the decision to eat a real meal. It's the decision to step outside and feel the wind. I am alive, and today, that is enough. I am counting every win, no matter how small. I am building a ladder out of "today" so I can reach "tomorrow."

## 26. The Reclaiming (Reclaiming Joy)

I forgot what I liked. For a long time, I was just surviving, and joy felt like a luxury I couldn't afford—like trying to buy a yacht when you can't pay the rent. But now, I'm going back for the things the depression stole. I'm listening to music again, and I'm actually *hearing* it, not just using it as background noise for my misery. I'm tasting my food. I'm laughing at things that are actually funny, not just because it's my turn to laugh.

Joy isn't a destination; it's a practice. It's the decision to notice the light when it hits the leaves. It's the decision to pet the dog or buy the flowers or sing in the car. I'm reclaiming my right to be happy, even if it's just for five minutes at a time. I'm realizing that I don't have to be "perfectly healed" to enjoy a sunset. Joy is allowed to exist alongside the struggle. I'm opening the windows and letting the air in. I'm inviting the light back into the room, one small spark at a time.

# 27. The Circle (Finding Your Tribe)

I found people who speak my language. They don't look at me like I'm a problem to be solved; they look at me like a person to be loved. Finding your tribe is about realizing you don't have to explain your "weird" or your "dark" to the right people. They already know. They've been there. We are a collection of broken mirrors reflecting the light for each other, turning the shards into a mosaic.

I am no longer an island. I am part of a circle, and the circle is strong enough to hold us all. We don't judge the bad days; we just bring over the soup and sit in the silence. We celebrate the "shower wins" and the "therapy breakthroughs." I'm learning that vulnerability is the glue that keeps us together. When I stop hiding, I find that I'm not alone. I'm part of a community of survivors, a tribe of people who know that the "architecture of the mind" is a collective project. We are building each other up, one conversation at a time.

# 28. The Daily Work (Living with It/ Maintenance)

Healing isn't a "done" state. It's not a destination you reach and then stay forever. It's a daily choice. It's the vitamins, the walks, the therapy, the "no"s, and the "yes"es. It's maintenance. Like a car or a house, the mind needs upkeep. You don't just clean the house once and expect it to stay clean forever. You have to sweep. You have to do the dishes. You have to fix the leaks when it rains.

I am learning to monitor the oil and check the tires. I am learning the warning signs of a "leak" before the whole basement floods. I am learning that I can live a full, beautiful life *and* have mental health challenges at the same time. They aren't mutually exclusive. I am a driver with a finicky engine, but I'm still the driver. I'm learning the rhythm of my own maintenance. I'm giving myself grace on the days when the work is hard. I'm realizing that the "work" is just another way of saying "I'm worth the effort."

# 29. The Oak Tree (Resilience)

I've been through the storm, and I'm still standing. I might have fewer leaves than I did before, and some of my branches are scarred from the lightning, but my roots go deeper than they ever did before. Resilience isn't about being "tough" or "unbreakable"; it's about being flexible. It's the ability to bend in the wind without snapping. It's the ability to grow back after the fire.

I am a testament to my own survival. Every bad day I've ever had—every "I can't do this" moment—I have a 100% success rate of getting through. That's a pretty good record. I am built to last. I am an oak tree in a world of storms. I am finding strength in the scars. I am realizing that the things that tried to break me only made my foundation stronger. I am proud of my survival. I am proud of my growth. I am standing tall, with my branches reaching for the sun and my roots holding fast to the earth.

# 30. To the One I'm Becoming (Letter to the Future)

Dear Future Me, I hope you're breathing easy today. I hope you remember the weight of the ink and the lightness of the clouds. I hope you're still writing, still feeling, still growing. I did the hard work so you could have the peace. I sat in the "Heavy" so you could enjoy the "Light." I walked through the fire so you could enjoy the glow. I want you to know that I am proud of you, even if you're having a bad day.

Don't forget where we came from, but don't feel like you have to live there anymore. You are not your past. You are the architecture of everything I dreamed of while I was sitting in the dark. Keep building. Keep opening the windows. Keep loving yourself without conditions. You are a miracle of survival and a work of art in progress. I love you. I'm glad we made it. Keep going.

# About the Author

Jashaun is a 17-year-old author from North Carolina who writes with raw honesty about his journey through mental health. His work reflects the struggles, strength, and self-discovery of a young mind navigating complex emotions. Through storytelling, Jashaun hopes to connect with others who feel unseen and remind them that their voice - and their story - matters.

www.ingramcontent.com/pod-product-compliance
Lightning Source LLC
LaVergne TN
LVHW022325200926
848481LV00004B/1437